Jim Beckwourth

ADVENTURES OF A MOUNTAIN MAN

Jim Beckwourth

ADVENTURES OF A MOUNTAIN MAN

by Louis Sabin
illustrated by Marion Krupp

Troll Associates

Library of Congress Cataloging-in-Publication Data

Sabin, Louis.
    Jim Beckwourth: adventures of a mountain man / by Louis Sabin;
illustrated by Marion Krupp.
       p.   cm.
    Includes index.
    Summary: Examines the life and career of the nineteenth-century
hunter, trapper, and trader.
    ISBN 0-8167-2819-4 (lib. bdg.)   ISBN 0-8167-2820-8 (pbk.)
    1. Beckwourth, James Pierson, 1798-1866—Juvenile literature.
2. Pioneers—West (U.S.)—Biography—Juvenile literature.
3. Trappers—West (U.S.)—Biography—Juvenile literature. 4. Afro-
American pioneers—West (U.S.)—Biography—Juvenile literature.
5. Afro-American trappers—West (U.S.)—Biography—Juvenile
literature. [1. Beckwourth, James Pierson, 1798-1866.
2. Pioneers. 3. Afro-Americans—Biography.] I. Krupp, Marion
Needham, ill. II. Title.
F592.B393S23 1993
978'.02'092—dc20   92-8717
[B]

Jim Beckwourth

ADVENTURES OF A MOUNTAIN MAN

"Eastward I go only by force; but westward I go free," the great American author Henry David Thoreau wrote almost two hundred years ago. Back then, the West was unmapped territory from the Mississippi River to California. For anyone brave enough and ready for adventure, it was rich in opportunity. A person's past didn't matter. In the West, only what you were and what you could do meant anything. It was a world that was perfect for someone like Jim Beckwourth.

James Pierson Beckwourth was born on April 26, 1798, in Fredericksburg, Virginia. His father, Jennings Beckwourth, was a major in the Revolutionary War. After the war he became a farmer. Jim was the third of Jennings Beckwourth's thirteen children. Jim's mother was a slave.

In those days there was no way for a black-and-white family to live free in Virginia. So Mr. Beckwourth moved his family out West. They settled on land between the fork of the Mississippi and Missouri Rivers, twelve miles from St. Charles, Missouri.

Beckwourth's Settlement covered hundreds of acres, with fields, streams, woods, and a mill for grinding corn. Some of Beckwourth's Settlement was leased to tenant farmers. These families, along with the Beckwourths, made up a small community.

The people living in the settlement worked together in many ways. They helped each other put up houses, clear the land, and provide defense against bands of troublemakers. To protect themselves, the settlers built blockhouses. Blockhouses, which are a kind of fort, were located wherever three or four farms met. The families that lived on these farms were all responsible for building the blockhouse, keeping it in repair, and posting a guard. When a guard saw signs of danger, he rang an alarm bell. This was a signal for everyone to hurry to the blockhouse to defend their homes.

Jim Beckwourth was seven years old when his family founded the settlement. One of the first things he learned was to hunt. There were bears and wildcats in the forest, as well as deer, turkeys, and rabbits. "There's plenty of game, Jim," Mr. Beckwourth said time and again. "And it doesn't take much craft to bag all you need. What takes sense is to get your game . . . and see that nothing gets you. A hunter must use his eyes and ears all the time."

Mr. Beckwourth gave his children a thorough frontier education. Every one of his seven sons and six daughters learned to ride, shoot, work the land, feed the stock, track game, cook, and fish. Mr. Beckwourth taught his children which wild leaves and fruits were safe to eat, how to use the sun and the stars for direction, and how to read and write.

Mr. Beckwourth was an unusual man for his time. He believed that skin color, religion, and a way of life didn't make one person better than another. When Jim once made a nasty remark about a Native American boy, Mr. Beckwourth said, "Hold on, son. Don't ever forget that your mother was a slave in Virginia. They can't see her as a person because she's black. And they can't see you as a person for the same reason. They're wrong, and what you said is just as wrong. You have to accept all kinds of people."

But when Jim was nine years old, his faith in people was put to a hard test. As he wrote, years later, "One day my father called me to him, and asked me whether I thought myself man enough to carry a sack of corn to the mill. The idea of riding a horse and visiting the mill thrilled me, and I replied with a hearty yes . . .

"About midway to the mill lived a neighbor with a large family of children, with whom I often joined in boyish games. On my way I rode joyously up to the little fence which separated the house from the road, thinking to say hello to my play-mates. What was my horror at discovering all the children, eight in number, from one to fourteen years of age, lying in various positions in the door-yard, dead and scalped. In the door-way lay their father, and near him, their mother, in the same condition; they had all shared the same fate. I found myself soon back at my father's house, but without the sack of corn—how I managed to get it off I don't remember—and described everything to my father."

14

Mr. Beckwourth rounded up ten other settlers and they set out to catch the killers. "In two days the band returned," Jim wrote, "bringing with them eighteen Indian scalps; for the backwoodsman fought in Indian style, and it was scalp for scalp between them."

Young Jim was shocked and angry. He wondered why anyone murdered innocent people. "I'll never understand," Jim said to his father.

"Well, son, you have to understand," Mr. Beck-wourth said. "There's another side to this. I think what that murderous bunch did to your friends was wrong as can be. But most Indians are decent human beings."

17

Mr. Beckwourth took Jim for a long walk. "Let's look at the way the Indians live," Mr. Beckwourth said. "They've been here a mighty long time, long before we came." The Native Americans, he explained, lived by hunting and trapping wildlife. They went wherever the hunting was good. They stayed in one place only during the winter. They had no fences, no permanent houses.

"That's not wrong, Jim, it's just different from our way. But now, put the two of us together—the Indian and the settler—and there's a problem. We say, 'It's our land, keep off!' They say, 'The land belongs to the whole tribe. It's a gift of the Great Spirit.' To them it's evil to keep some people from using what the Great Spirit gave to all."

It was still hard for the boy to understand why people killed each other. But he did understand one thing—there was good and bad on both sides, Native American and settler.

In 1808, when Jim was ten years old, he was sent to school in St. Louis. In the four years he attended school, the boy learned reading, writing, arithmetic, and history. He studied the Bible and read some of Shakespeare's plays. Jim liked the adventure-filled stories he read, and he dreamed of living a hero's life.

Jim stayed with a St. Louis family his father knew from Virginia. Every day after school, he went to the riverfront before going home. There was always something new to see. St. Louis was a busy trading place for merchants, trappers, Native Americans from many different tribes, and adventurers from all parts of the world.

Jim liked to watch the blacksmith shoeing horses, and rivermen poling their flatboats, mackinaws, and keelboats through the water. He listened to languages from all over the world, among them French, Spanish, German, and Portuguese. And there were the Native Americans from the North, West, and Southwest, speaking Flathead, Nez Perce, Sioux, Crow, Snake, Pawnee, and many other languages.

Jim had a fine ear for language. He soon picked up enough foreign words to speak some and understand a lot more. And he had a keen eye for the way different people behaved. He learned many things: that it was impolite to refuse food offered by a Native American; that it was dangerous to ask personal questions of a trapper or riverman; that it was smart to keep your hands still and out in the open when you were with strangers. All this was an education not found in the schoolhouse.

When Jim was fourteen, he left school and became an apprentice to George Castner, a St. Louis blacksmith. Jim spent the next five years working for Mr. Castner and living in his home. In time, Jim became an able blacksmith and developed a powerful set of muscles. Smithing was tough, sweaty work, but he never minded that. He liked doing physical things. He said it made him feel alive.

Jim also liked living in St. Louis. It was a lot more exciting than Beckwourth's Settlement. He enjoyed going home a few times a year to visit his family and friends. But a week on the farm was more than enough. Jim knew he wasn't cut out to be a farmer.

As much as Jim liked St. Louis and blacksmithing, he was growing eager for something new. Every night after work he went down to the riverfront. The stories he heard there put wonderful pictures in his head. He met such unbelievable characters that he hated to leave them and go home. One night, Jim stayed out so late that he got in trouble with his boss. Mr. Castner made it clear that his rules didn't allow late hours and bad company.

"Follow my rules, Jim, or leave my house," Castner said.

Jim scowled. Castner picked up a hammer and threw it at the young man.

"I dodged the missile, and threw it back at him in return," Jim wrote in his autobiography. "A scuffle followed, in which I, being young and athletic, came off master of the ground. I then accepted his dismissal and walked out, never to return."

Jim went home and told his father what had happened. Mr. Beckwourth advised Jim to go back and apologize to Mr. Castner. Jim said, "No! Never!"

"In that case, stay here," Mr. Beckwourth said. "I'll set you up in your own smithy."

Jim politely turned down the offer and, as he wrote, "declared a growing wish to travel. Seeing my determination, my father finally consented to my departure. He wished me well, gave me five hundred dollars in cash, together with a good horse, saddle, and bridle, and bade me God speed upon my journey."

It was the spring of 1818 when twenty-year-old Jim Beckwourth signed on with an expedition led by Colonel Richard M. Johnson. The expedition's aim was to work out a treaty with the Sac Indians. The Sacs lived along the Upper Mississippi River in what is now Iowa, Illinois, and Wisconsin. There were lead mines in Sac territory. Colonel Johnson wanted the Sacs to allow settlers to work those mines.

The expedition set out with about one hundred men, heading upriver in eight keelboats. It took nearly a month to reach a mine site called Fever River. Fever River was just a collection of tents set on a bluff above the Mississippi. To reach the village from the Mississippi, Beckwourth and his companions had to climb ladders leaning against the steep side of the bluff.

Fever River's miners lived a harsh life. They cooked outdoors and slept in abandoned mine-shafts in the winter and flimsy tents in the summer. The village was a filthy mud hole, and many of the miners fell sick with typhoid fever.

Colonel Johnson and his aides parleyed with the chiefs of the Sac and Fox tribes. After nine days of talk a treaty was signed. It gave mining rights to the settlers in exchange for supplies and a promise of peace. A celebration followed, with lots of dancing, merrymaking, and eating.

This was Beckwourth's first opportunity to spend time with Native Americans, and he enjoyed it. Eating with his new friends was unforgettable. The main dish was buffalo, and just about every part of the animal was eaten. The Native Americans made soup with buffalo blood and bone marrow, and snacked on the raw liver and gall bladder. Then came the roasted ribs and boiled steaks. Finally, buffalo sausages were served. A buffalo sausage was one long link roasted in the fire. When the sausage was ready, it was thrown on a blanket. It was immediately set upon by those who weren't already stuffed with food. Sometimes two feasters started at opposite ends of a coil of sausage and worked their way toward the middle. Each ate faster and faster while their friends cheered them on.

The feast ended when there was no more food. Only then was it proper for Johnson's expedition to leave for home. But Beckwourth wasn't ready to go. He was enjoying himself too much. For the next two years he lived with the Sacs. As he wrote, "The Indians soon became very friendly to me, and I was indebted to them for showing me their choicest hunting-grounds. There was abundance of game, including deer, bears, wild turkeys, raccoons, and numerous other wild animals."

Yellow Face, a Sac brave, taught Beckwourth how to trap beaver and otter. Beaver and otter pelts were very valuable. Fur traders paid so well for them that the pelts were sometimes called "hairy banknotes." They were worth from three to six dollars apiece, a lot of money at that time.

Yellow Face showed Beckwourth how to make an underwater trap with a smooth pole about ten feet long. It took hours of patient, careful work to prepare and set each trap. But it was worth it, for the traps worked well. Beckwourth was grateful to Yellow Face for this valuable lesson.

Beckwourth also spent time working in the lead mines. As he wrote, "I saved up seven hundred dollars in cash, and feeling myself to be quite a wealthy personage, I decided to return home."

It was the fall of 1820 when Beckwourth reached the family settlement. But he didn't stay long. A few months later he was back in Indian territory, hunting and trapping. He went home for another short stay, followed by a trip downriver to New Orleans, then back home again. There were two things that kept Beckwourth from staying at home. He loved the adventure he found in Indian territory. And he wanted to stay a free man.

Every time Beckwourth returned to St. Louis or the settlement, he was in danger of being arrested as a runaway slave. Jennings Beckwourth went to the Missouri Circuit Court in St. Louis three times to file papers for his son. Each time Mr. Beckwourth swore that James was a free man. Even so, Jim Beckwourth's safety was never certain. Slavery didn't end until the Civil War was fought, forty years later.

On October 11, 1823, Beckwourth went to work for William Henry Ashley's Rocky Mountain Fur Company. He and twenty-eight other trappers in the party rode out of St. Louis for the beaver-rich central Rockies. Ashley outfitted the group and guaranteed he would pay well for every pelt they brought back. And he hired the veteran trapper Jedediah Smith to lead the party.

Until now, trappers had traveled along the route laid out by the Lewis and Clark Expedition in 1804. But there were other routes through the Rocky Mountains, and Native Americans from many tribes had used them for hundreds of years. Smith's group decided to look for one of those unmapped trails. They headed west along the Platte River, finally crossing the towering Rockies at South Pass. They were the first non-Native Americans to go west through the pass.

In Smith's party were Jim Bridger, Kit Carson, Jim Beckwourth, Pierre Louis Vasquez, Thomas Fitzpatrick, Edward Rose, Jim Clyman, and Milton Sublette. They became known as the Mountain Men. Fearless adventurers, they achieved fame guiding wagon trains and U.S. Army troops across the West. They were like living maps for all who followed them.

The Mountain Men existed in two worlds at once—the Native American's and the settler's. They spoke the languages of many tribes, as well as English, French, and Spanish. This made them valuable to Native Americans, traders, Army officers, and wagon-train trail bosses.

Beckwourth worked for the Rocky Mountain Fur Company for ten years. Each fall he went into the mountains with a small party of trappers. They collected as many pelts as possible before the cruel winter set in. Then they hid their bundles of fur out of the reach of animals and headed for their cold-weather camps. Some Mountain Men holed up in valleys sheltered from the icy winds and heavy snows. Others, who were married to Native American women, joined their wives' tribes for the winter.

When the spring thaw began, the animals became active again. So did the trappers. They added many more pelts to their stockpile. Finally summer came, bringing Rendezvous time. Rendezvous was a meeting of trappers and the traders they worked for. It took place at a convenient location known to everyone. In later years many famous trading posts and Army forts were built on old Rendezvous sites. Some of these grew into cities.

At Rendezvous, the traders paid for the pelts in cash. The Mountain Men paid their debts and bought supplies for the coming year. Then it was time for celebrating. There were wrestling and boxing matches, horse- and foot-races. There was gambling, dancing, eating and drinking, fights, and endless story-telling. By the time Rendezvous was over, most of the trappers were deeply in debt again.

Beckwourth usually came out of Rendezvous completely broke. He dreamed of settling down someday, but it was many years before he was able to save enough money to retire.

Beckwourth and the other Mountain Men kept on trapping, but they took fewer pelts each year. The number of fur-bearing animals was growing smaller. And things were changing. Settlers were coming in, putting up fences. With them came bigotry, the kind that had made Beckwourth's life impossible in St. Louis.

In 1834, Jim Beckwourth and Jim Bridger were trapping along the Big Horn River, in what is now Wyoming. The two trappers were working about a mile apart when Beckwourth was surrounded by a party of Native Americans. Bridger heard their voices and climbed a hill to see what was happening. He saw Beckwourth being led away by the Native Americans. Bridger was sure that Beckwourth was as good as dead. And that is what he told fellow trappers at the next Rendezvous.

Bridger was wrong. Beckwourth's captors were Crow. This tribe was friendly with the trappers. Beckwourth was led into the Crow village, where he was greeted warmly by Long Hair, the tribal chief. Beckwourth was surprised. He had spent time in Native American villages before and never had any problems. But this was different—he was being treated like a long-lost son!

The reason was simple. Another chief, Big Bowl, said Jim *was* his son. Years before, Big Bowl's young son was kidnapped by an enemy tribe. Everyone was very sad until a wise counselor told Big Bowl, "Do not grieve. One day your son will return. He will be a fine brave, and will bring you much honor. Now he is hunting in the South, where the sun blazes long and hot."

When the Crows saw Jim Beckwourth's dark skin, they remembered the counselor's words. They said the sun had burned Beckwourth's skin to its dark color. Surely this powerful man was Big Bowl's lost son. This idea appealed to Beckwourth. He liked getting so much love and respect.

Beckwourth was called "Bloody Arm," which was the kidnapped boy's name. The Crows gave him a lodge of his own, as well as horses, clothing, weapons, and other gifts. Then he was married to Pine Leaf, Chief Long Hair's daughter. Finally, James P. Beckwourth was made a chief of the Crows.

Mistaken identity may have made Beckwourth a chief, but his courage and common sense made him a worthy member of the tribe. In the years that followed, the Crows faced many attacks from the Cheyennes, Pawnees, Snakes, and other enemies. As Native American territories grew smaller, tribes were pushed closer together. Their food supply shrank. These conditions led to wars between tribes. In every attack against his tribe, Beckwourth fought bravely as the leader of his band of warriors. Big Bowl was proud of his "son"!

Beckwourth never lost his itch for adventure. When he got restless, he saddled his horse and headed out of the village, promising to return. Sometimes he hired on as a guide for a wagon train heading to Oregon territory. Sometimes he acted as a scout for the U.S. Army. Beckwourth's travels took him in all directions. He rode along the Santa Fe Trail, through the Southwest and into Mexico. He traveled the Oregon Trail, and up into the Canadian Rockies.

Beckwourth's name became a permanent part of American history in April 1850. He was prospecting for gold in the Sierra Nevada Mountains, along the California-Nevada border, when he noticed a distant valley. It looked deeper than all the others in view. Beckwourth marked it in his mind. Then he rode back to the California camp, put together provisions, and set out with another prospector.

It was near the end of April when Beckwourth found his valley. It was rich with flowers and grass. He wrote, "Swarms of wild geese and ducks were swimming on the surface of the cool crystal stream . . . or sailed the air in clouds over our heads. Deer and antelope filled the plains, and their boldness [made it clear] that the hunter's rifle was to them unknown . . . It is probable that our steps were the first that ever marked the spot."

The route Beckwourth pioneered is marked on maps as Beckwourth Pass. And the valley, where he settled in 1852, is still called Beckwourth Valley.

46

Beckwourth and his wife, Pine Leaf, built a
trading post in Beckwourth Valley, and lived
there for the next ten years. Then they sold the
property in 1862 and retired to a small ranch near
Denver. It was there, sometime in October 1866,
that sixty-eight-year-old Jim Beckwourth died.

Mountaineer, scout, pioneer, Crow chief—James
P. Beckwourth was a rough, tough dreamer-
adventurer whose eyes were always fixed on the
horizon . . . and beyond. Westward he went free,
and made his mark on America.

INDEX